PROPERTY OF
ST. CLEMENT'S
LIBRARY
ROSEDALE, MD.

SPACE JOKES

Compiled and Illustrated by
Viki Woodworth

Text copyright © 1991 by The Child's World, Inc.
All rights reserved. No part of this book may be
reproduced or utilized in any form or by any means
without written permission from the Publisher.
Printed in the United States of America.

Distributed to Schools and Libraries
in Canada by
SAUNDERS BOOK COMPANY
Box 308
Collingwood, Ontario, Canada 69Y3Z7 / (800) 461-9120

Library of Congress Cataloging-in-Publication Data
Rothaus, James.
Space jokes / Jim Rothaus; compiled and illustrated by Viki Woodworth.
p. cm.
Summary: A collection of jokes about the planets and outer space.
Example: What kind of fur do you get from an Alien?
As fur away as possible.
ISBN 0-89565-730-9
1. Outer space—Juvenile humor. 2. Riddles, Juvenile. 3. Wit and humor, Juvenile.
[1. Outer space—Wit and humor. 2. Jokes.]
I. Woodworth, Viki, ill.   II. Title.
PN6231.S645R68 1991   91-18578
818'.5402–dc20   CIP / AC

SPACE JOKES

Compiled and Illustrated by
Viki Woodworth

A man asked for a ticket to the moon.
"Sorry," the ticket seller said, "The moon is full right now."

Which stars wear minks and drive fancy cars?
Movie stars.

What's the difference between a loaf of bread and the sun?
One rises from yeast and the other rises in the east.

What did the Martian find when he landed in the ocean?
Water.

What do little Space Creatures get when they're good?
Gold stars.

How often do you see blue Aliens?
Once in a blue moon.

What did the Martian cook in his skillet?
Unidentified frying objects.

What type of baseball game is held in a planetarium?
The All-Star Game!

Which planet makes the most noise?
Saturn, it has rings.

What did the Martian say when it felt flypaper?
I'll stick with you.

How do you talk to a giant Alien?
Use big words.

Who has orange fuzzy hair, a painted mouth and floats in the sky?
Bozo the Cloud.

At a space exhibit a model spaceship disappeared. A note was left in its place.
It said: "Goodbye, earth people. Thanks."

How do you stop an Alien baby from crying?
You rocket (rock it).

What's the best way to call an Alien?
Long Distance.

Did you hear the new joke about the sun?
"No."
"I'd better not tell you. It's over your head."

What do you do with a green Alien?
Let it ripen.

Where did Mickey Mouse go in the spaceship?
To visit Pluto.

How do you stop a 257-lb Martian from charging?
Take away its credit cards.

When was beef the highest?
When the cow jumped over the moon.

How does a lamb get to the moon?
By rocket sheep.

1st Kid: I saw something last night I'll never get over.
2nd Kid: What?
1st Kid: The moon.

When does the moon need money?
When it's down to its last quarter.

Who was the first settler in the West?
The sun.

What space adventurer is really a deer?
Buck Rogers.

How does an Alien get clean?
In a meteor shower.

What is an astrologer's favorite soup?
Capri-corn chowder.

What kind of umbrella does an Alien use when it's raining?
A wet one.

What do Martians have that no one else has?
Baby Martians.

An Alien asked a sparrow to direct him to a hotel. "Cheep, cheep," said the sparrow.
"It better be, getting here cost a fortune."

What's crazy and flies to the moon?
A loony module.

What kind of steps do astronauts take when they meet Martians?
Very, very, big ones.

How will you have the best space flight?
Planet (plan it).

Alien: Will you join me in a cup of coffee?
2nd Alien: Do you think we'll both fit?

What dance does a cow do on the moon?
The mooooon walk.

What comes from space and plays music.
A Martian band.

A flying saucer landed in New York, but didn't stay. Why not?
No parking places.

Sign at Cape Kennedy:
Out to launch.

Who gives parking tickets in outer space?
A meteormaid.

Where do Aliens go after they get married?
To a honeymoon.

What did the 6-legged Alien say to her dance partner?
You're stepping on my foot, my foot, my foot, . . .

What would you get if you crossed a vampire bat and a magician?
A flying sorcerer.

What is a solar hat?
A sunbonnet.

Where are dead Aliens listed?
In the orbit-uaries.

Where do astronauts store their wallets?
In air pockets.

What happens when a 12-ton Martian goes to Burger King?
He has it his way.

Why did the Space Creature stick his finger in the light socket?
To catch up on current events.

What do you call a crazy astronaut?
An astro-nut.

What do you get when a huge Space Creature lands in your garden?
Squash.

Spaceman: It's not supposed to rain today!
Other: Why not?
Spaceman: Because today is Sunday.

What did the Martian say when he landed in a garden?
Take me to your weeder.

What is a sheep that eats grass in space?
A star grazer.

How do you spell Alien backwards?
A-l-i-e-n-B-a-c-k-w-a-r-d-s.

How does an Alien count to 67?
On his fingers.

What astronaut needed braces on his teeth?
Buck Rogers.

Which stars are the most dangerous?
Shooting stars.

What is the name of the star with a tail?
Mickey Mouse.

If you flew to the sun, when would you not burn up?
At night.

Why is an astronomer's business always good?
It's always looking up.

What kind of surface does a football field have in outer space?
Astroturf.

How does Darth Vadar cook stir-fries?
In ewoks.

How did the sailor find out there is a man in the moon?
He went to sea.

How do space cowboys talk to each other?
With communication saddle lights.

Athletes get athletes' foot, so astronauts must get mistletoe.

Martian: That girl rolled her eyes at me.
Other Martian: Well, roll them back to her.

When cows fight in outer space, what is it?
Steer wars.

How can you find out if a Martian can count?
Ask it what three minus three is and see if it says nothing.

How do you make an Alien stew?
Keep it waiting for a long time.

How do you make an Alien shake?
Run up behind it and yell "Got'cha."

What did the Martian say to the gas pump?
Take your finger out of your ear and start talking.

What kind of bug lives on the moon?
Lunar tick.

What keeps the moon in the sky?
Moon beams.

How do you make a Martian float?
Two scoops of ice cream, some soda and a Martian on top.

What is the first day of a Martian's week?
Moonday.

What potato went into orbit?
Spudnik.

What do you call an Alien that eats people when they aren't looking?
Shy.

The law of gravity keeps us on earth, so what did people do before that law was passed?

How can the astronomer see stars in the daytime?
By hitting himself on the head.

How can you tune into the sun?
Turn its sundial!

What did the Martian say to the flea?
Let's go out for a bite.

What do Martians eat on Mars?
Mars mallows.

Who was the wierdest captain of the Starship Enterprise?
Captain Quirk.

What did the Martian say to the egg?
Take me to your beater.

Who gets congratulated when they're down and out?
Astronauts.

Earth: How are your craters?
Moon: Very depressed.

When the sun is tired, what does it do?
It sets awhile.

Why is a shooting star like a fat cow?
It's meteor (meatier).

When do Martians take it easy?
On Saturnday and Sunday.

What did the Alien say to the soda bottle?
Take me to your liter.

How do you greet a two-headed Martian?
Hello! Hello!

Why does the moon go to the bank?
To change quarters.

How do they pour milk into the Milky Way?
With the Big Dipper.

Which is heavier the sun or the earth?
The earth, the sun rises every morning.

How did the Alien start a flea market?
From scratch.

What do astronauts eat from?
Flying saucers.

What movie has Darth Vadar living in New York?
The Empire State Building Strikes Back.

1st Alien: You have beautiful eyes.
2nd Alien: Thank you. They were a Christmas present.

How can you tell if an Alien is a boy or a girl?
Give the Alien a candy bar. If he eats it, it's a boy, and if she eats it, it's a girl.

When seventeen Aliens begin yelling, biting and beating each other up, what time is it?
Party time.

What's the difference between a Space Creature and peanut butter?
A Space Creature doesn't stick to the roof of your mouth.

Did you hear the story of the Alien who ate New York?
Never mind—you wouldn't swallow it..

What kind of fur do you get from an Alien?
As fur away as possible.

Alien Mother: Should we take Junior to the zoo?
Alien Father: No. If the zoo wants him, they can come for him.